8/11
21.99

DICTATORS AND TYRANTS

STORIES OF RUTHLESS RULERS

by Michael Burgan

Consultant:
Rodd Freitag
Associate Professor of Political Science
University of Wisconsin, Eau Claire

CAPSTONE PRESS
a capstone imprint

Velocity is published by Capstone Press,
151 Good Counsel Drive, P.O. Box 669, Mankato, Minnesota 56002.
www.capstonepress.com

092009
005620LKS10

Books published by Capstone Press are manufactured with paper
containing at least 10 percent post-consumer waste.

Library of Congress Cataloging-in-Publication Data
Burgan, Michael.
    Dictators and tyrants : stories of ruthless rulers / by Michael Burgan.
    p. cm. — (Velocity. Bad guys)
    Includes bibliographical references and index.
    Summary: "Provides short biographies of some of history's most infamous dictators and tyrants,
detailing their desire for power and their violent ways" — Provided by publisher.
    ISBN 978-1-4296-3423-6 (library binding)
    1. Dictators — Biography — Juvenile literature. 2. Heads of state —
Biography — Juvenile literature. 3. Kings and rulers — Biography — Juvenile
literature. I. Title. II. Series.
D107.B83 2010
321.9092'2 — dc22   2009032778

Photo Credits
Alamy/The London Art Archive, 12
AP Images, cover (bottom left)
The Bridgeman Art Library/©Look and Learn/Private Collection/McConnell, James Edwin, 11
Corbis/Bettmann, 21; Hulton-Deutsch Collection, 14 (right); Hulton-Deutsch Collection/Eugene
    McCarthy, 31
Getty Images Inc./AFP, 29, 33, 36; AFP/AFP, 38; AFP/Srdjan Sulejmanovic, 44 (top); AFP/STR, 39;
    The Bridgeman Art Library, German School, 8; The Bridgeman Art Library/Victor Mikhailovich
    Vastnetsov, 10; Hulton Archive/Imagno, 23; Keystone, 34; National Geographic/David A. Harvey, 37;
    Popperfoto/Paul Popper, 19; Time Life Pictures/Thomas Hartwell, 40
The Granger Collection, New York/ullstein bild, 18
International Institute of Social Geschiedenis (History) IISG/Stefan R. Landsberger Collection,
    http://chineseposters.net, 30
iStockphoto/James McQuillan, 9 (garlic, wooden stake, and a cross); Liz Leyden, 35
Landov LLC/dpa, 16 (top)
Library of Congress, 15, 22 (top), 28; Geography and Map Division/CIA 1990, 42, 44 (bottom)
NARA/DVIC, 20 (WWII soldiers); Heinrich Hoffman Collection, 24 (German police); Joc Shaw, 41;
    Lt. A.E. Samuelson, Army, 25; Peterson, Army, 32; Pfc. W. Chichersky, Army, 26 (ovens);
    SSGT Jeremy T. Lock, USAF, 43
Newscom/Rapport Press/Morten Hvaal, 45; UPI Photo/Sergey Starostenko, 27 (back)
Shutterstock/Ann Triling, cover (bottom right); c., 7 (coins); CreativeHQ, 20 (grenade);
    ElenArtFoto, 16 (bottom); Eric Isselée, 13; frescomovie, 5 (tank); Galushko Sergey, cover (top);
    Jim Vallee, 22 (bottom), 25 (swastika); Jonathan Larsen, 4, 7 (coliseum); Micimakin, 24 (book);
    Olemac, 5 (helmet & ammunition); riekephotos, 26 (star patch); Rolandino, 4 (helmet);
    Vlad Ageshin, 27 (front); Zorik Galstyan, 14 (left)
SuperStock, Inc./SuperStock, 6 (Nero)

Design Elements
Shutterstock/Ann Triling, (fist); easyshoot, 6, 7 (background); Galushko Sergey, (planes);
    High Leg Studio (dragon); Hintau Aliaskei, (frames), (tape); Jozsef Szasz-Fabian, (Castle);
    Vasyl Helevachuk (gold frames)

TABLE OF CONTENTS

ALL-POWERFUL LEADERS

About 2,500 years ago, the Greeks created the word *tyrannos*. It describes a person who took power and ignored citizens' **rights**.

Hundreds of years later, the Romans sometimes gave power to one person during an emergency. They called this person a dictator.

right

a basic freedom for the people that rulers should obey and protect; the freedoms of speech, press, and religion are rights.

Today we call rulers who have complete power tyrants or dictators. The deadliest leaders have appeared in modern times. Inventions like tanks, airplanes, guns, and harmful chemicals help these rulers kill many people quickly.

Tyrants and dictators control TV, radio, and newspapers. They often use **propaganda** to control public opinion. Most tyrants and dictators use the fear of arrest, torture, or death to make sure their citizens obey them. These rulers also have people who spy on citizens. Their spies read other people's mail and listen to phone conversations. They even keep track of citizens who leave the country.

Many tyrants and dictators have a twisted sense of right and wrong. They are often driven by desires for control, revenge, or personal gain. They convince themselves that what they want is best for their people, even if it means causing them harm. These all-powerful leaders often cause unbelievable devastation.

propaganda

biased, incomplete, or false information that is spread to influence the way people think

NERO

37 – 68

Rome had many unpopular emperors. Nero was probably the most hated of all. He became emperor in the year 54, at the age of 17.

Nero watching a gladiator match

Nero would do anything for wealth and power. He took land from citizens and ordered the owners killed. Nero killed anyone who seemed to threaten his power. He ordered the deaths of his mother, stepbrother, and one of his wives.

At times Nero killed out of pure cruelty. He had one wife killed simply because he disliked her. When another wife angered Nero, he kicked her, even though she was pregnant. The blow killed her and the unborn baby.

In the year 64, a fire swept through Rome. Many Romans suspected that Nero set it so he could rebuild the city the way he wanted. Nero falsely accused local Christians for the blaze. He tortured and killed many of them.

After the fire, Nero's enemies planned to kill him. Nero learned of the plot. He killed many of those plotting against him. But soon the army turned against Nero. He knew he could not survive as emperor. Nero killed himself before his enemies could kill him.

VLAD THE IMPALER

1431 – 1476

In 1456, Vlad Dracula took control of Wallachia, a part of modern-day Romania. Vlad was called "the Impaler." He often had enemies and criminals **impaled**.

Vlad had many enemies who wanted to take over as ruler of Wallachia. He used violence to scare them and show his power.

FACT:

Dracula's father, Vlad Dracul, was a member of a group of knights called the Order of the Dragon. His name meant "Vlad the Dragon." Dracula means "son of the dragon."

impale

to thrust a sharpened stake through a person's body

Vlad's main rivals were the Turks. He fought many battles against them to keep the throne of Wallachia. Vlad lost and regained it three times.

Vlad also used violence against his own people. He claimed it was for the good of the country. The penalty for committing even a minor offense was impalement. During his rule, Vlad ordered the deaths of up to 100,000 people through impalement. Vlad's victims included women and children.

symbol of
the Order of the Dragon

FACT:

Vlad also wanted to rid his country of illness and poverty. But his method for doing this was cruel. Vlad invited a large group of poor and sick people to a banquet. Then he locked them inside the hall and burned it down. Vlad's cruel reign finally ended when he died in battle in 1476.

Bram Stoker's novel *Dracula* was published in 1897. He named his character Count Dracula after Vlad Dracula. Vlad, of course, was not a vampire. But his many gruesome murders suggest he enjoyed seeing the blood of others.

cross

garlic

wooden
stake

legendary weapons used against vampires

IVAN THE TERRIBLE

1530 – 1584

Ivan IV became tsar, or ruler, of Russia in 1547. During his rule, he killed thousands of his own people. It was no wonder Russians called him "Ivan the Terrible."

FACT:

Even before he was tsar, Ivan showed his cruel streak. Fearing the power of several **boyars**, he killed them. One was impaled. Another had his head chopped off.

To ensure his power, Ivan used a secret police force to hunt down his enemies. He had enemies slaughtered and then took their land. Ivan had some of the boyars strangled or drowned.

boyar

a member of the Russian nobility who is in line for the throne after the royal family

Ivan's worst mass killings came in 1570. The city of Novgorod had a history of self-government. Ivan was suspicious that these citizens were trying to break away from his rule. Ivan sent his police force to demolish the city of Novgorod. His men killed thousands of the city's wealthy and powerful people. Thousands more citizens froze or starved to death after the attack.

Ivan's last major murder was in 1581. In a rage, he hit his own son over the head with a large rod. Ivan died three years later of unknown causes.

MAXIMILIEN ROBESPIERRE

1758 – 1794

In the 1780s, the country of France was deep in debt. Many people were poor and hungry. Angry citizens blamed these problems on the way the king and queen ran the country. These citizens wanted to have more control in government.

In 1789, **rebels** forced France's king from power. By 1793, Maximilien Robespierre was one of the rebels' leaders.

The rebels had many enemies inside and outside of France. Robespierre believed arresting and killing these foes was the only way to keep power. He helped unleash a "Reign of Terror" across the country.

rebel

a person who fights against the established government

People who seemed to threaten the rule of the rebel forces were arrested. Many were killed. The killings started with France's former royalty. As the terror spread, priests, merchants, and peasants were also arrested.

In 1794, Robespierre supported a law allowing the government to execute people without proving their guilt. Thousands were killed with the **guillotine**.

As executions grew more frequent, citizens panicked. It seemed the slightest mistake could send someone to the guillotine. People were starting to think that Robespierre had gone too far.

In his last speech, Robespierre claimed to have a list of traitors. But he refused to hand over the list. Afraid their names may be on the list, other leaders arrested Robespierre. They sent him to the guillotine, as he had done to so many people before him.

guillotine

a large machine with a sharp blade used to cut off heads

13

ISMAIL ENVER PASHA

1881 – 1922

Ismail Enver Pasha was one of Turkey's main leaders during World War I (1914–1918). He helped carry out the **genocide** of Turkish Armenians.

Enver Pasha and other Turkish leaders wanted to expand their country, uniting other Turkish-speaking Muslim nations. But the Armenians, who were Christian, lived in the middle of the area the Turks wanted to conquer. Enver Pasha's solution to this problem was to get rid of the Armenians altogether.

genocide
to intentionally destroy a race of people

ruins of an Armenian Christian church

The genocide began in the fall of 1914. Enver Pasha removed all Armenians from the army. He forced them to build roads for the government. Many died from being overworked. The rest were killed once their work was complete.

The government soon ordered the removal of all Armenians from the country. The Turks forced millions of Armenians out of their homes. The Armenians were forced to march hundreds of miles to the desert of Syria. Thousands of Armenians died from thirst and hunger. Thousands more were killed by the Special Organization, a military group controlled by Enver Pasha.

Most of the people who died on the march to Syria were women and children.

Armenian refugees

Enver Pasha died fighting in Russia in 1922. He remains a symbol of Turkish cruelty. Turkish leaders still refuse to admit their government killed more than 1 million Armenians.

JOSEPH STALIN

1879 – 1953

In 1917, Russian **communists** overthrew their tsar and the current government. The communists renamed Russia and the surrounding occupied countries the Soviet Union. Joseph Stalin became one of the Soviet Union's most powerful leaders. When the main leader, Vladmir Lenin, died in 1924, Stalin took control of the country.

communist

a member of a political party who believes in a form of government in which all land, homes, and businesses belong to the government, with the profits shared by all

Vladmir Lenin's image on a Russian coin

In 1929, Stalin began putting farms under government control. In the Ukraine, many people fought Stalin's effort to take their farms. In 1932, Soviet officials took grain from Ukrainian farmers to punish them. Several million Ukrainians starved to death. Others were killed by government officials.

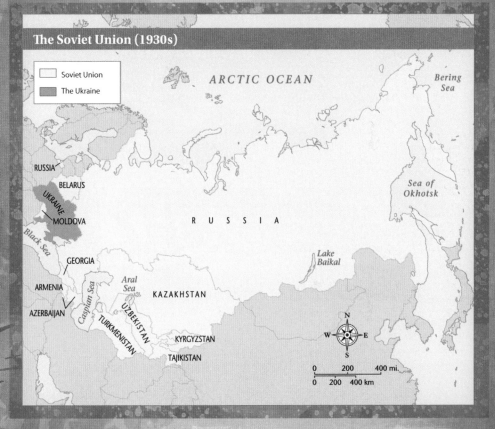

The Soviet Union (1930s)

Soviet Union
The Ukraine

ARCTIC OCEAN

Bering Sea

RUSSIA

BELARUS

UKRAINE

MOLDOVA

Black Sea

GEORGIA

ARMENIA

AZERBAIJAN

Caspian Sea

Aral Sea

KAZAKHSTAN

UZBEKISTAN

TURKMENISTAN

KYRGYZSTAN

TAJIKISTAN

R U S S I A

Lake Baikal

Sea of Okhotsk

N
W   E
S

0   200   400 mi.
0   200   400 km

Stalin's secret police force hunted down anyone who might oppose him. Throughout the 1930s, the secret police tortured and killed Soviet communists who threatened Stalin's rule. Others were sent to prison camps. Some of these people had once been Stalin's supporters.

Stalin's effort to get rid of possible enemies is known as the Great Terror. During 1937 and 1938, Stalin personally ordered the deaths of 40,000 people. Together, he and his supporters killed about 1 million Soviet citizens during those years.

prisoners working in a gulag

The Gulags

Stalin did not kill all of his enemies. He sent some of them to prison camps called gulags. Most of the camps were in Siberia. Siberia was a cold and remote part of the Soviet Union. The prisoners were forced to work outside in the bitter cold. They often lacked food, and many froze to death.

Guards did not bother to help sick or injured workers. Instead, they left them to die. Guards also beat prisoners who did not finish their work. Most prisoners lacked the energy to work hard because they had so little food. From 1934 to 1953, as many as 25 million people died in Stalin's gulags.

In August 1939, Stalin signed a treaty with German leader Adolf Hitler. The two dictators agreed not to attack each other. Secretly, they also agreed to conquer and divide up Poland.

Soviet "Red Army" on the march

Soviet troops soon invaded Poland and Finland. Stalin also took control of Latvia, Lithuania, and Estonia. In many of these countries, the Soviets took land by force and killed local leaders who opposed them. Two million Poles were sent to Siberia.

During World War II (1939–1945), Stalin blamed the deaths of several thousand Polish prisoners of war on Germany. The killings took place in a part of Russia called the Katyn Forest.

The truth was that Stalin had ordered the killings. Almost 22,000 captured Poles were executed at Katyn and in nearby villages.

In June 1941, Hitler broke his agreement with Stalin. Germany invaded the Soviet Union. Millions of Soviet troops helped defeat Germany in World War II. During the war, Stalin told his troops to kill fellow soldiers who did not fight.

German troops attacking Soviets

After the war, Stalin spread Soviet influence. He helped communists take power in Poland, East Germany, and other parts of Eastern Europe. The communists arrested and killed political enemies. When Stalin died in 1953, the Soviet Union controlled most of Eastern Europe. Stalin is remembered as one of the cruelest mass murderers in history.

FACT:

Stalin's cruelty even extended to his family. During World War II, the Germans captured his son, Yakov. But Stalin refused to try to get him back. Stalin then had his son's wife arrested and sent to a prison camp.

Yakov Stalin (center) being arrested

ADOLF HITLER

1889 – 1945

On September 1, 1939, Germans soldiers stormed into Poland. World War II had begun because of the evil dreams of one man — Adolf Hitler.

Hitler had fought for Germany in World War I. The Germans lost that war and were forced to give up land and money. Hitler was furious about how these demands had weakened Germany. He wanted to make his country powerful again.

Hitler believed many people threatened Germany, especially Jews. Hitler wrongly believed they were inferior people. This belief is called anti-Semitism.

Hitler also believed the Germans formed a master race and that they should rule over Europe. This idea eventually led Hitler to start World War II.

During the 1920s, Hitler became head of the **Nazi Party**. Eventually, he became the leader of Germany. But the German people did not vote Hitler into office. In 1933, the German government created a law that gave Hitler control over the country.

Germans saluting Nazi officers

There were many political parties in Germany at the time. The Nazis were the most popular of all the parties. But they did not have the support of the majority of Germans. The Nazis had to force most Germans to obey them.

Nazi Party

the German political party led by Adolf Hitler; the name was short for National Socialist German Workers' Party.

Hitler had a security force called the SS. He also created a secret police force called the Gestapo. Gestapo officers spied on Germans to make sure they followed Nazi orders. Citizens who did not were arrested or killed.

German police entering Austria

ADOLF HITLER
mijn kamp

FACT:

In 1923, Hitler tried to take over the German government, but his revolt failed. He was arrested and sent to prison. There Hitler wrote a book called *Mein Kampf*, which is German for "My Struggle." It outlined his plans to take power in Germany and rob the Jews of their freedom.

In 1933, the Nazis began using concentration camps to hold Jews and other people seen as undesirable. They rounded up people by the thousands and sent them to the camps.

Life in the concentration camps was brutal. Prisoners were sometimes jammed so tightly together that they had no room to lie down at night. They barely received enough food to keep them alive. After working all day, the prisoners were sometimes forced to stand for hours in the rain or freezing cold.

concentration camp prisoners

Guards sometimes beat prisoners for such things as putting their hands in their pockets. Many prisoners died from the beatings or the hard work they were forced to do.

Camp Experiments

Hitler saw nothing wrong with making the Jews suffer. In some camps, Nazi doctors used the Jews in terrible medical experiments. Prisoners were exposed to deadly diseases to see how their bodies would react. Some female prisoners had parts of their leg bones removed. In one experiment, prisoners sat in tubs of cold water. Doctors wanted to see how long they could bear the low temperature.

In 1941, Hitler decided to create camps for the sole purpose of killing Jews. This horrible genocide is known today as the Holocaust.

death camp ovens

In the death camps, the Germans used poison gas to kill large numbers of Jews at once. The dead bodies were then burned in huge ovens.

Sometimes the Germans didn't even bother with the camps. They simply rounded up Jews and forced them into vans. Once inside, they were gassed. Other times, the Germans shot them by the thousands. Their bodies were then stacked in ditches. Guards fired guns into the piles to make sure everyone was dead. On September 29 and 30, 1941, more than 33,000 Jews from Kiev, Ukraine, were killed this way.

gate to Auschwitz concentration camp

Jewish memorial in Kiev

Altogether, 6 million Jews died during the war. Hitler's policies killed many other people as well, including disabled people and political opponents.

Hitler killed himself on April 30, 1945. He had realized that Germany could not win the war. The details of the horrible acts Hitler ordered came out in trials held after the war. His name still calls to mind the slaughter of millions of innocent people.

MAO ZEDONG

1893 – 1976

During the mid-1900s, Mao Zedong led China, the world's most populated country. He had a great vision for the future of his country. But in trying to reach his goals, Mao proved to be one of the cruelest dictators ever.

Mao wanted to build a communist society in China. During the 1920s and early 1930s, he led Chinese communists in a civil war against Chinese who opposed them. The communists won the war in 1949.

Mao would do anything to keep control over China. He wanted people to fear him so that they would obey him. During and after the civil war, he executed people who opposed his ideas. He had them killed in public and forced local people to watch.

communist tank in Shanghai, China

FACT:

Mao hated taking baths. Instead, he had guards wipe his body and hands with hot towels. He also did not brush his teeth very often. His personal doctor wrote that Mao's teeth were covered with a green film. When the doctor touched his gums, pus came out of them.

Once in control of China, Mao set up prison labor camps. His enemies were arrested and sent to the camps without being given a fair trial.

Prisoners worked hard and received little food. Guards would beat prisoners who were too weak to do their jobs.

industrialize

to set up businesses and factories in an area

In 1957, Mao began what he called the Great Leap Forward. He wanted China to **industrialize**. Mao killed more than 500,000 people who opposed his plan. He also forced farmers to work in factories. But without farming, the country ran out of food. Nearly 40 million Chinese starved. The Great Leap Forward ended in failure in 1961.

A few years later, Mao turned on his own people. He thought educated people threatened his rule. The effort to eliminate them was called the Cultural Revolution. It lasted from 1966 into the 1970s.

During this time, millions of young Chinese left school to join the Red Guard. This was Mao's special police force. Its young members were taught to adore Mao. They wanted all Chinese people to worship him like a god.

female soldiers in the Red Guard

Red Guard members forced teachers, scientists, and government leaders to leave cities and work on farms. Mao also let Red Guard members kill and torture people who seemed to threaten his rule. About 1 million people died during the Cultural Revolution.

Mao died in 1976. He had tried to keep the worst parts of his rule a secret. Today, the world knows the horrors Mao committed.

KIM IL SUNG

1912 – 1994

After World War II, Korea was divided into northern and southern sections. Kim Il Sung soon emerged as the leader in the North. He created a tightly-controlled communist state. Kim killed North Koreans who challenged his rule.

American soldiers during Korean War

Kim also attempted to take over South Korea. He began the Korean War (1950–1953). American forces fought on South Korea's side. Together, the two countries defeated North Korea.

After his defeat, Kim quickly rebuilt his country. He forced many North Koreans to work on farms. The government took over almost all property.

North Koreans were made prisoners in their own country. Kim also kept most foreigners out of North Korea. He controlled the media, limiting what North Koreans learned about their country and the rest of the world.

Kim died in 1994, and his son Kim Jong Il took over. Together, the two Kims have made millions of their own people suffer so they could rule with total power.

Kim Il Sung (left) and Kim Jong Il (right)

Like Father Like Son

Like his father, Kim Jong Il has punished anyone who opposed him. He also has kept North Korea cut off from the world. During the 1990s, millions of North Koreans starved during a **famine**. But Kim Jong Il refused to seek the world's help. Kim also built up North Korea's military. He even broke an agreement not to build nuclear weapons. Some world leaders fear Kim could use the weapons or sell them to terrorists.

famine
a serious shortage of food resulting in widespread hunger and death

IDI AMIN

1925 – 2003

Idi Amin began his military career as a Ugandan soldier. Aggressive and ambitious, he quickly rose through the ranks to the highest position possible. In 1971, he led the Ugandan forces in an attack against their own president. Amin seized power of Uganda and began his violent reign. His goal was to obtain wealth and power.

Under Amin, the Ugandan army and special police controlled the country. They often arrested and beat people for no reason. They demanded money from the victims in exchange for their release. Sometimes victims were taken away and never seen again.

In Uganda's jails, guards beat prisoners to death or strangled them. The bodies of some of the dead were fed to crocodiles.

Amin and his thugs killed about 500,000 Ugandans. Some people thought Amin was crazy. Others said he used violence to create fear. If the people were afraid of him, they would not challenge him.

FACT:

People who fled Uganda said that Amin had killed his wife and ordered her body cut up.

In 1979, Ugandan **exiles** and the Tanzanian army finally drove Amin from power. He fled Uganda and was never punished for the terror he caused.

exile

someone who is sent away from his or her own country and ordered not to return

POL POT

1928 – 1998

Pol Pot seized control of Cambodia in April 1975. He led a communist group called the Khmer Rouge. Pol Pot and his military forces ended up killing 1.7 million of his own people.

Pol Pot (far left)

The Vietnam War (1959–1975) led to Pol Pot's rise to power. U.S. planes often attacked North Vietnamese bases in Cambodia. These attacks also killed many Cambodians.

Pol Pot blamed the Cambodian government for those killings. He convinced many Cambodians to help him take over the government. Pol Pot wanted to create a communist government in Cambodia, with farming as the country's main source of wealth.

Once in power, Pol Pot demanded total loyalty to his government. To control information, he shut down the media and burned books. He even took children away from their parents. That way, the government could influence the children's thoughts.

mass grave of victims of the Khmer Rouge

Pol Pot feared that both foreigners and his own people would try to end his rule. He ordered all foreigners to leave the country. Any who remained were killed.

Pol Pot's next move was to cut off all contact with the rest of the world. Any Cambodians who spoke foreign languages or had worked for other countries were arrested or killed.

forced evacuation of a Cambodian city

Cambodian prisons were brutal. Prisoners were whipped with electrical wire or bamboo branches called rattan. The prisoners confessed to crimes they did not commit just to end the torture. After confessing, many were killed.

Under Pol Pot, Cambodians could only work for the government. The government forced people to farm. The Khmer Rouge closed all schools and businesses. They forced several million people to leave Cambodia's cities and move to farms.

Pol Pot made the people work 18 hours every day. The farmers barely received enough food to live. Armed soldiers watched them at all times. Some guards slit the throats of Cambodians who disobeyed orders. People also died from starvation and disease. These farms earned the name "the killing fields."

The Cambodians had to travel on foot when they were forced to leave the cities for the countryside. The Khmer Rouge even forced sick people to leave hospitals and roll down streets in their beds. As many as 20,000 people died during these forced marches.

workers in the killing fields

In December 1978, Vietnam invaded Cambodia. They forced Pol Pot from power. He and the Khmer Rouge fled to the countryside. Pol Pot died in the jungles of Cambodia in 1998.

SADDAM HUSSEIN

1937 – 2006

Saddam Hussein took control of Iraq in 1979. He soon became a menace to both neighboring countries and his own people.

In 1980, Hussein launched an invasion of Iran. During the war, he ordered his troops to shoot captured Iranian soldiers. Hussein also killed as many as 20,000 Iranians using chemical weapons.

Hussein even killed his own people. The Kurdish people are one of Iraq's main ethnic groups. Between 1980 and 1988, the Kurds sided with Iran in the war against Iraq. When the war ended in 1988, Hussein brought revenge against the Kurds. That year alone, his soldiers killed more than 100,000 Kurds.

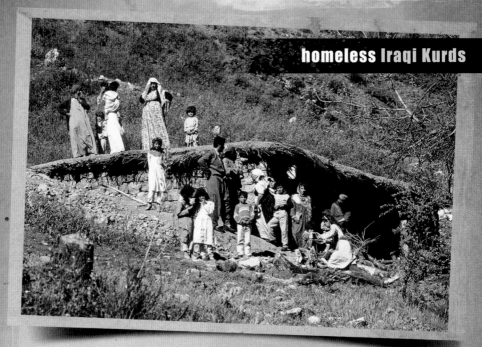

homeless Iraqi Kurds

The Gassing of Halabja

On March 16 and 17, 1988, the residents of the mostly Kurdish Iraqi village of Halabja looked up to the sky. Overhead, Iraqi warplanes dropped bombs filled with deadly gases. The gases killed some people instantly. Others began to vomit and their skin started to burn. Shortly after, many of them died too. Hussein's attack on Halabja was one of the worst mass killings in history. As many as 5,000 people died in the attack. Another 10,000 were wounded.

According to Hussein, the only way to keep his power was to arrest citizens who opposed him. He ordered some prisoners to be killed soon after going to jail. Others were tortured. Guards gouged out some prisoners' eyes and gave others electrical shocks.

Middle East, 1981

In 1990, Hussein went to war again. His forces invaded Kuwait. The next year, the United States and 33 other nations joined together to help Kuwait. Together, their forces drove the Iraqis out of Kuwait. This conflict was called the Gulf War.

At the end of the war, Iraqi members of a religious group called Shiites rebelled against Hussein. He struck back by killing thousands of them.

During the Gulf War, Hussein stored weapons under schools, hospitals, and other public buildings. He hoped his enemies would not risk killing innocent people by attacking those sites.

After the Gulf War, the United Nations punished Iraq. They limited what goods the country could receive from other countries. Iraq was still allowed to buy food. Hussein sold some of this food and kept the money for himself. Many Iraqis went without food and medicine. In the meantime, Hussein spent $2 billion to build dozens of palaces across the country.

In 2003, the United States led an invasion of Iraq to remove Hussein from power. He was captured and sent to jail. Hussein was executed in 2006 for killing innocent civilians. He will be remembered as one of the most heartless dictators in world history.

SLOBODAN MILOSEVIC

1941 – 2006

Slobodan Milosevic was sometimes called the "Butcher of the Balkans." He ruled a part of Yugoslavia called Serbia. Yugoslavia split apart in the 1990s. During this time, Milosevic caused a great deal of bloodshed.

Yugoslavia

Croatia and other parts of Yugoslavia wanted independence. Milosevic opposed them. Some Yugoslav generals supported Milosevic. In 1991, they invaded part of Croatia where many Serbs lived. Yugoslav soldiers and tanks destroyed the city of Vukovar, killing many Croats.

Milosevic's next move was to try to stop Bosnia from becoming independent. He helped get weapons for Bosnian Serbs who were fighting Bosnian Muslims and Croats.

Albanians in Kosovo also wanted their independence. Again, Milosevic opposed this idea. In 1998, Milosevic's forces began forcing Albanians from their homes. They killed as many as 10,000 people. International troops led by **NATO** finally forced Milosevic to end the killings.

Milosevic was put on trial for war crimes. Many people were convinced of his guilt. Milosevic would probably have been executed, but he didn't live long enough for it to happen. Milosevic was still on trial when he died in 2006 from heart problems. Unfortunately, he is probably not the last violent dictator the world will see.

fighting in Sarajevo, Bosnia

FACT:

The Serbs carried out what is called "ethnic cleansing." This means killing or removing all people who belong to a certain ethnic or religious group. In Kosovo, Slobodan Milosevic murdered up to 1.5 million Albanians.

NATO

a group of countries including the United States and Britain that help each other defend themselves; NATO stands for North Atlantic Treaty Organization.

GLOSSARY

boyar (BOY-uhr) — a member of the Russian nobility and one of the next in line for the throne after the royal family

communist (KAHM-yuh-nist) — a member of a political party who believed in a form of government in which all land, homes, and businesses belonged to the government; the profits were shared by all.

exile (EG-zyl) — a person who has been sent away from his or her own country and ordered not to return

famine (FA-muhn) — a serious shortage of food resulting in widespread hunger and death

genocide (JEN-oh-side) — to intentionally destroy a race of people

guillotine (GEE-uh-teen) — a large machine with a sharp blade used to cut off heads

impale (im-PALE) — to thrust a sharpened stake through a person's body

industrialize (in-DUHSS-tree-uh-lize) — to set up businesses and factories in an area

NATO (NAY-toh) — a group of countries including the United States and Britain that help each other defend themselves; NATO stands for North Atlantic Treaty Organization.

Nazi Party (NOT-see PAR-tee) — the German political party led by Adolf Hitler; NAZI is short for National Socialist German Workers.

propaganda (prop-uh-GAN-duh) — biased, incomplete, or false information that is spread to influence the way people think

rebel (REH-buhl) — a person who fights against a government

right (RITE) — a basic freedom based on morals and usually protected by laws; free speech and freedom of religion are rights.

READ MORE

Dowswell, Paul. *Dictatorship.* Systems of Government. Milwaukee: World Almanac Library, 2006.

Geyer, Flora. *Mao Zedong: The Rebel Who Led a Revolution.* National Geographic World History Biographies. Washington, D.C.: National Geographic, 2007.

Haugen, Brenda. *Joseph Stalin: Dictator of the Soviet Union.* Signature Lives. Minneapolis: Compass Point Books, 2006.

Rice, Earle. *Blitzkrieg! Hitler's Lightning War.* Monumental Milestones. Hockessin, Del.: Mitchell Lane, 2008.

INTERNET SITES

FactHound offers a safe, fun way to find Internet sites related to this book. All of the sites on FactHound have been researched by our staff.

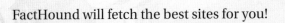

Here's all you do:

Visit *www.facthound.com*

FactHound will fetch the best sites for you!

INDEX